FESTIVAL FOLK

FESTIVAL FOLK

A celebration of the unique style of
Fairport Convention's Cropredy Festival

Photographs
Joss Mullinger

Words
Catherine Hayward

Foreword
Simon Nicol

Profits from the sale of this book will be donated to the Teenage Cancer Trust
(registered charity no 1062559)
supported in recent years at the Cropredy Festival.

FESTIVAL FOLK

First published in Great Britain in 2005 by This Way Books
PO Box 3224, Maidenhead, Berkshire SL6 6WW

Edited by James Mullinger, London
Designed by Glynn Grylls, Maidenhead, Berkshire
Scans by Snappy Snaps, Brook St, London W1S 1BB
Printed by BAS Printers, Salisbury, Wiltshire

ISBN 0-9549434-0-6

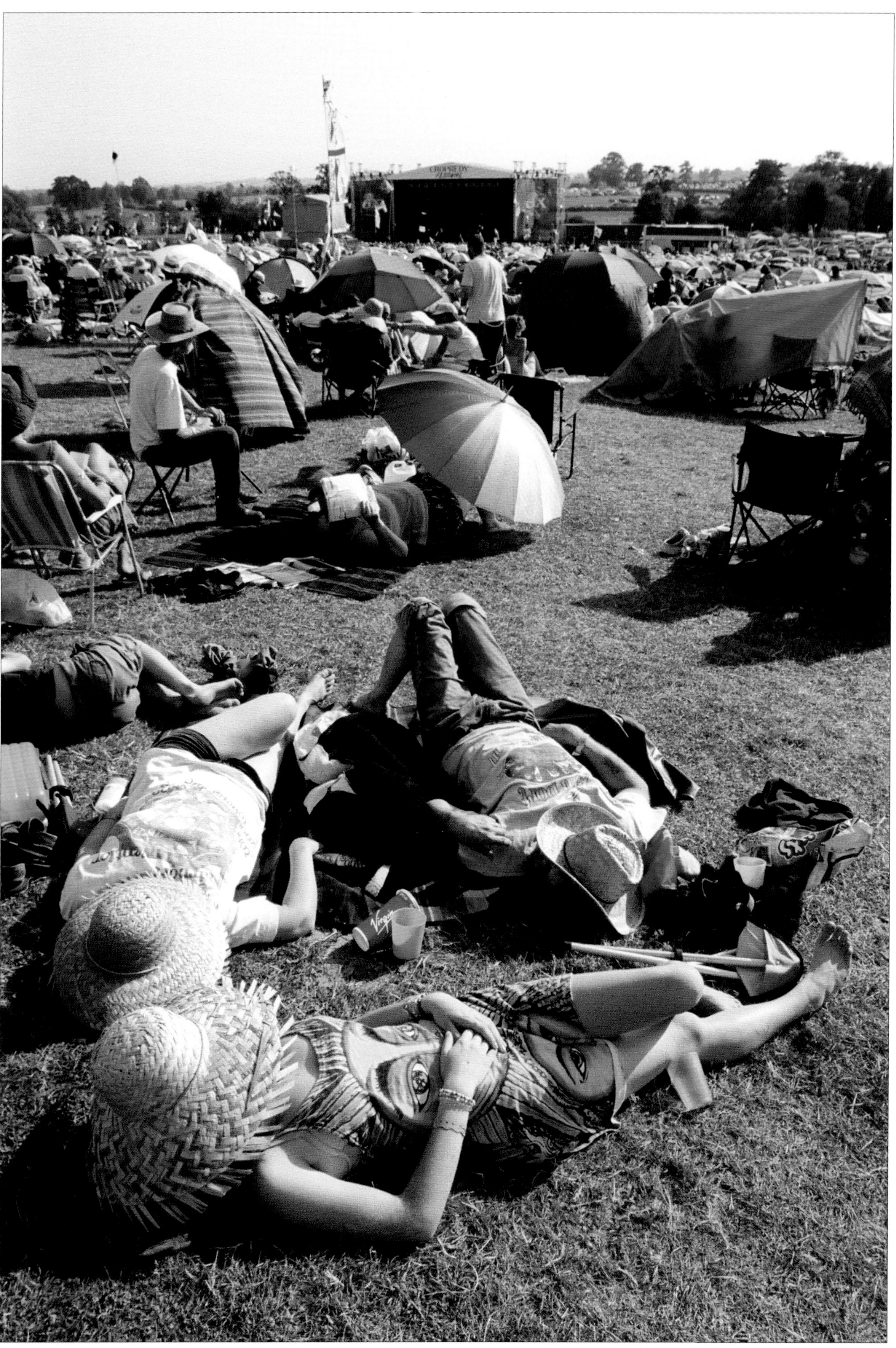
CROPREDY
Virgin

Foreword

by

Simon Nicol

As someone who has spent most of his adolescence and all of his adult life bound up with Fairport Convention (feel free to draw your own dividing line, dear reader), the annual gathering of the faithful and the idly curious at Cropredy is an occasion non pariel. The festival has grown quietly and steadily under the careful stewardship of Chris Pegg since its inception as a residents-only thank you to the village for the loan of their hall for rehearsals. At this time it was merely a chance to show the villagers what it was we did when we trundled off in the group van to distant parts only to shatter the small hours with our cheery "goodnights" and championship door-slamming on our return. From these humble beginnings the festival has become the biggest independently run event of its type and it is something I am hugely proud to be associated with.

Just as a professional photographer will have seen more snaps than Joe Bloke, I've seen more festivals than many of you: from the primitive idealistic shambles of the 1968 Isle of Wight through the boot-sucking Flanders mud of Dranouter to the sublime organisational excellence of the multimedia immersion of Woodforde, set on the edge of a Queensland rain forest and providing so much to so many. But I've never been anywhere with the ethos of our own event – where everyone has their own take on the band, the camping, the food and (sorry!) the VIBE...

While Fairport were briefly semi-retired in the early eighties, we referred to it as a reunion festival; and in a way, for the crowd, it still is; but the reunion is now between these disparate souls who once a year come from their real lives in Taunton or Tokyo, Mannheim, Manchester or Melbourne to meet up in a North Oxfordshire field and share something intangible.

And as you'll see from Joss' eloquent photographs they bring a lot of themselves and their flair to the party. I feel I know many of these people - indeed I could name several of them - and it's good to sit here and reconvene in the winter and look forward to seeing them again next summer in all their colourful finery!

Simon Nicol
co-founder of Fairport Convention

December 2004

Introduction

As a veteran of many festivals in the 'golden era' between 1968 and 1973 ranging from the National Jazz & Blues events (at Kempton Park, Plumpton and the fledgling Reading rock), the 1970 Bath festival, Weeley, Phun City and others, I returned to the throng in 1994 at Fairport Convention's Cropredy Festival to find the eclectic appearance of the festival audience had not diminished in the intervening years.

The now legendary Cropredy festival originated from a farewell event organised by the founders of folk-rock music 'Fairport Convention' and has developed over the years into an annual three day musical family gathering for up to 20,000 people. It has taken place every August for over 25 years at the village of Cropredy, near Banbury in Oxfordshire.

Impressed by the diverse appearance of the audience as well as the performers, I set out with my camera to record over the next ten years the sights and styles and to capture the colourful atmosphere and 'joie de vivre' expressed visually by many festival goers.

In this work I have concentrated mainly on the audience although the members of Fairport Convention and other artists have also earned their place as will be seen in the final chapter entitled 'Style on Stage'.

The audience is a much neglected element in music related publishing and this work is intended to redress the balance by concentrating on the overall style of festival folk, paying particular attention to details such as their hair styles, hats, beards(!), body art, jewellery and T-shirts. I have included a mixture of the young, the not-so-young, the ordinary, the funsters and the bizarre – all the elements that contribute towards the vividly colourful celebration that is the world's best loved folk-rock festival.

Along with the older 'Fairport' fans, many people have grown up with the festival and now with their own children in tow, continue to experience the combined pleasures of camping, mud and music. It is noticeable that at music festivals more orientated towards the teens & 20's, the street fashions of the day tend to predominate – this younger crowd wearing mostly the ubiquitous t-shirt & jeans, assorted versions of grunge or elements of the latest high street trends. At Cropredy however, the much wider age range means that a greater variety of clothes can be seen reflecting the more diverse music and social scenes. In many ways, it can be considered that a sense of style or fashion anarchy has emerged illustrated by the amazing variety and mixture of all elements of attire.

Just one feature is omnipresent – current and previous year's festival T-shirts tend to dominate the scene. The older the shirt, the more significant the statement of the wearer that 'I've been coming here since 19--'. The festival has been running since the late 1970's so there is plenty of scope for variety, assuming the design hasn't faded through countless washings. There is also a variety of slogan or emblem T-shirts, some of the more notable ones being designed by small groups of friends which identify their allegiance to both their group and the festival.

Despite this festival originating from the founders of folk-rock music, there appears to be no specific 'folk fan' style. The most significant and ubiquitous link between the traditional 'folkie' and the average Cropredy festival goer is a love of good English ale and this is evidenced by the number of personal tankards to be seen in hands or swinging from belt loops!

Unlike the modern British high street, at Cropredy hats are a major element in many peoples ensemble either to keep off the rain, to protect from the sun or an opportunity to show off something colourful and wonderful. The wide variety of headgear and expression of individuality on display at Cropredy can be seen in many of the photographs.

Turning now to the performers, the final chapter entitled 'Style on Stage' presents a small collection of performers. I make no apologies for the selection: current and past members of Fairport Convention appear alongside other performers who all meet the criteria of the book which is looking at festival fashions, colour & style. A great many performers have appeared in eye-catching, colourful or stylish apparel which has made the selection task difficult but I hope you approve of those included here.

So, whilst a specific folk fashion style does not particularly exist, in its place the festival folk emerge in all their glorious miscellany of colour and styles. In the next chapter, Catherine Hayward looks more closely at festival styles as an introduction to the photographs.

The subsequent pages pay tribute to everyone's unselfconscious colourful contribution to the festival scene and I hope the reader will enjoy basking in this recreation of the visual feast that is the unique atmosphere of Fairport Convention's Cropredy Festival.

Joss Mullinger

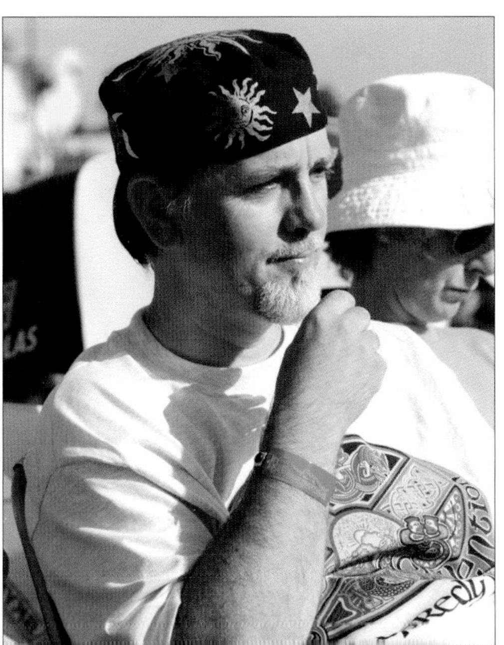

Acknowledgements

Firstly a big thank you to everybody included in this book. Your colourful contribution to the Festival helps to make it so special. My apologies to those people I photographed but who have not been included here, there was a lot of competition and space was limited – volume two perhaps?

This book would not have been possible without the hard work, flair and vision of everyone involved with creating and sustaining the festival over the years including Chris & Dave Pegg, the various members of Fairport Convention, everyone involved in the myriad of tasks in organising & running the festival, the many performers, the traders, the audience and the local residents. I would like to thank all these people and in particular, Chris Pegg and Simon Nicol for their support of my project.

Next I would like to thank my elder son James for editing my large collection of pictures and for his constant encouragement, Nick my younger son for his assistance with computer skills, Gary Cadogan for the initial design, Glynn Grylls for his skilled work in translating our ideas into the finished design, Donna Westley for her delightful celtic knot logo, and Catherine Hayward for her insight into fashion styles and entertaining observations. Andrew Hunter, Bobby Abbott and their colleagues at BAS Printers have been invaluable in assisting us through the overall process of printing.

Thanks are also due to Martin Bowrey, Thierry Bedue and Nick Herbert at the Brook Street 'Snappy Snaps' for their excellent photographic processing and scanning work.

I would also like to thank my friends & fellow festival goers: Phil & Jan, Anneliese, Kristina, Jane & Steve, Mark & Louise, Rako (the purple girl), Peter (no, you can't have my hat!) and Stuart for their encouragement and companionship every year in August.

Finally, I acknowledge and thank both my Mother who contributed towards the early colourful festival scene by sewing multi-coloured, triangular velvet inserts to flare my jeans (!) before my first festival in 1968 and my wife Margaret for her encouragement and patience during the long gestation of this project. You can have the dining room back now!

Further information about the festival can be obtained from
Fairport Convention's website
www.fairportconvention.com

To keep in touch register on their mailing list at
cannyconcerts@talk21.com
or write to Fairport Convention, 6 Stonehouse Business Centre,
Market Square, Chipping Norton, Oxon OX7 5NA

A four CD box set 'Cropredy Capers' which chronicles 25 years of
Fairport's annual Oxfordshire festival is available from Free Reed Music at
www.free-reed.co.uk

The book enclosed with the CD set is available separately from
Free Reed Music, along with their previous book 'Cropredy Chronicles'.

Festival Folk Style

by
Catherine Hayward

1996
1994

Festival Folk Style

by

Catherine Hayward

Funny lot, the British, To the rest of the world we sip tea at four in tweeds and brogues, our international identity clearly defined by a collective national reserve, a penchant for wellington boots and Barbours and the indefatigable stiff upper lip of Evelyn Waugh novels and kitchen sink dramas.

Put us in a muddy field with a tankard of ale, a picnic blanket and the promise of some entertainment, however, and you've got another story entirely.

Joss Mullinger's charming photographs tell that story. Against the backdrop of the annual Cropredy folk-rock festival in Oxfordshire, Joss' collection of frank, intimate photographs capture the spirit of true British individualism.

The images reproduced here are not the high fashion shots you see on the pages of high-maintenance glossy magazines. There are no designer labels, hi-tech fabrics or limited editions in evidence. No Prada, no McQueen, no Marks and Spencer even. And if there are, well, they're hidden beneath a well constructed veneer of dip-dyed shirts, hand-crafted bracelets and catweazle facial hair.

What we have here is style innovation in its purest form. Alternative, entrepreneurial and sometimes ever so slightly loopy. The festival goers depicted here aren't hugging trees exactly, they just know what they like and don't seem to care what anyone thinks. As long as they're noticed not caring, that is.

And that's the point. The embellishment, decoration and styling is designed not so much to impress as to get each individual as much attention as possible. Why else would you dye your hair purple and pierce your tongue? It certainly never did the Sex Pistols any harm.

I've been to a few gigs over the years: The Rolling Stones at Wembley; Blondie in Amsterdam; David Bowie at Milton Keynes Bowl: The Fall in Camden; hell, I'll even admit to 10CC at Crawley Leisure Centre in 1979. But nothing quite prepares you for your first festival. As I pitched my tent on an obscure hill in the middle of the Sussex Downs, cursing the heavy raindrops that slid silently down the back of my neck, I knew that 24 hours of musical oblivion lay ahead. Who cared if my socks were soaked through and I was developing trench foot. I'd seen the footage of Hendrix playing the Star Spangled Banner at Woodstock countless times; I'd marvelled at the frilliness of Mick Jagger's white shirt as he flailed manically on stage at their free Hyde Park concert in 1969 too; I'd even taken a passing shine to the deeply unflattering top worn by Janis Joplin at the Monterey Pop festival in 1967 – a long-sleeved, nylon A-line number that reminds me now of 'The Good Life's' Margot Leadbetter.

OK, I may only have witnessed these events by proxy but at my very own real life festival, I felt like one of Ken Kesey's Merry Pranksters and in my mind, our clothes – all vandalised denim and layers of psychedelic friendship bracelets – were as important as the vibe. As it happens, I can't remember any of the music that weekend. The speakers blew up and any attempt at crowd pleasing with acoustic versions of Led Zep's Communication Breakdown faded into another kind of oblivion after the third cider. What I do remember is the intriguing sight of the couple in front. She in the ubiquitous festival uniform of the 90s – combat pants, fleece and uber trendy trainers - and her attentive boyfriend in sturdy DMs, a full face of hair and a rather fetching purple floral dress.

The late sixties was the heyday of the big rock festival. It was a time of immense cultural upheaval – the Age of Aquarius - and the new generation of music fans was encouraged to 'tune in and drop out'. Fairport Convention emerged during this era of big acts like Hendrix, The Grateful Dead, Creedence Clearwater Revival, Pink Floyd and Traffic, and took full advantage of the new vogue for communal ambience.

But it wasn't until the mid 1970s that the band, previously dubbed a 'British Jefferson Airplane', organised the Cropredy festival to celebrate the continuing popularity of British folk music. With glam rock dead on its feet and punk on its last legs, the re-emergence of a folk rock festival must have been anathema to the burgeoning MTV/hip-hop generation about to burst on the scene. But re-emerge it did to enormous success and an annual attendance of up to 20,000 folk fans.

With his trusty Canon, Joss Mullinger's straightforward approach to his subject matter echoes the stark realism of influential US photographer Larry Clark. But it is humour that sets Joss' pictures apart. And like documentary photographer Martin Parr, well known for his quirky, realist take on life, Joss gets involved. There may be no hippies, punks or goths in his pictures; no chavs or sloanes or nu-metal fanatics; no grunge, no scallies, not even a specific folk style for that matter. What we get is a crazy car crash of images that is the glorious British audience dressed up to the nines for a weekend in a field. Psychedelic beads and batik prints; tie-dye shirts and tattooed biceps; western bandanas, medieval headgear or a jaunty embroidered fez. It's Tommy Cooper meets Jethro Tull at a Polyphonic Spree gig. And, of course, a very British take on fashion.

Photograph by Mark Lebon

Catherine Hayward

Fashion Director of Esquire magazine

The Festival Folk

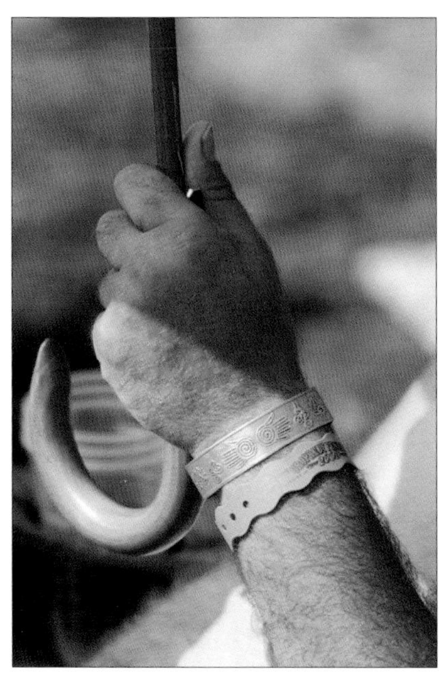

1999

2002

1999|2001
2002|1999

2004

2003

2003

1996|2000
1999|2000

2003
2002 | 2002
2003 |

2003

2003

2002 | 2004
2000 | 2002

2002

2003|2000
2002

2002

1999 | 1999
1999 | 2002

2003|2001
2002

2002|2002
1998|2002

2002

2003
2002 | 2003
1995

	2002	
2003	2002	1995
2003		1997

1995
2003 | 2003
1996

2004

1999
1995

1995	2004
2003	2003
1995	2000

2003
2000
2000

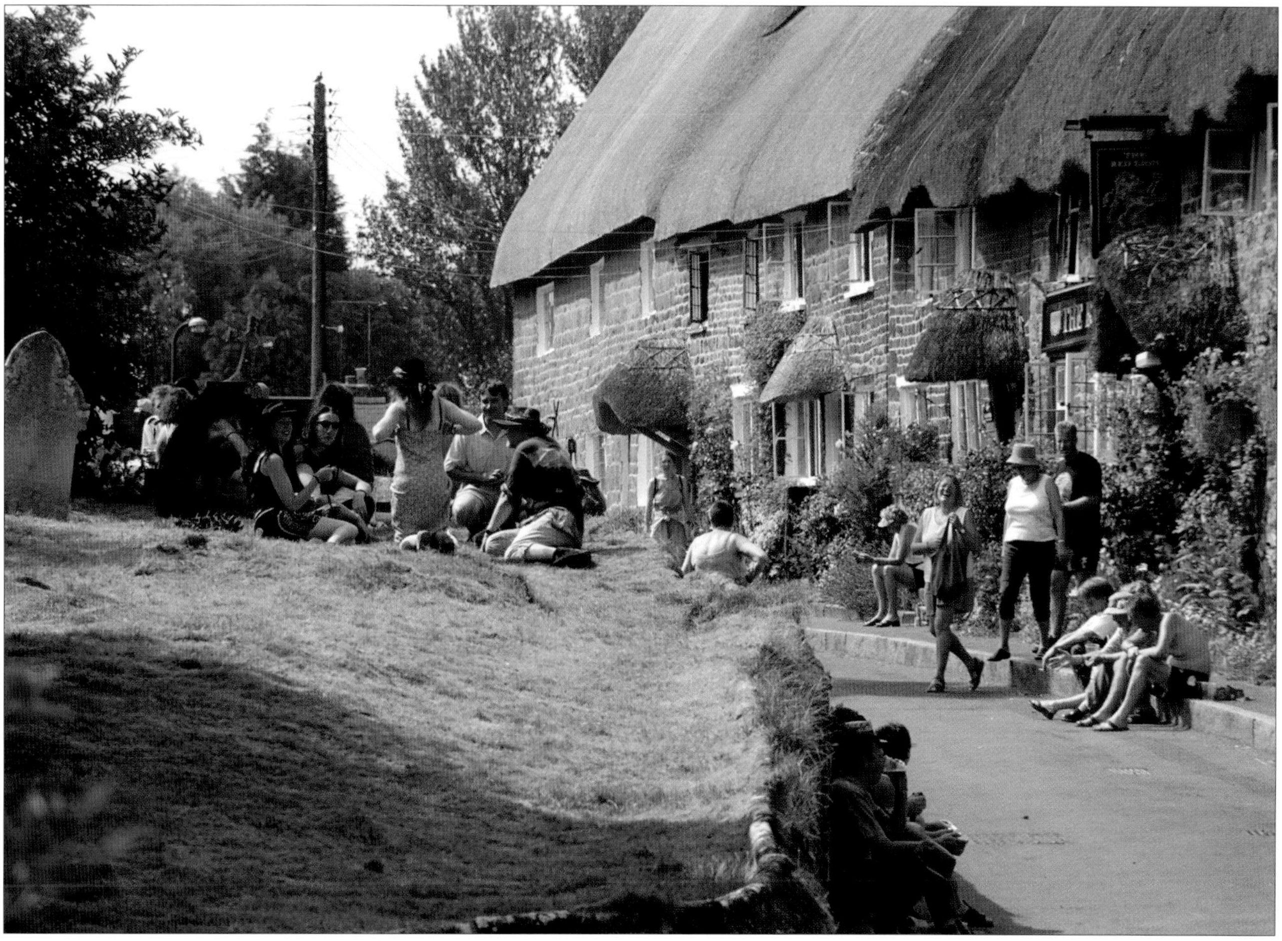

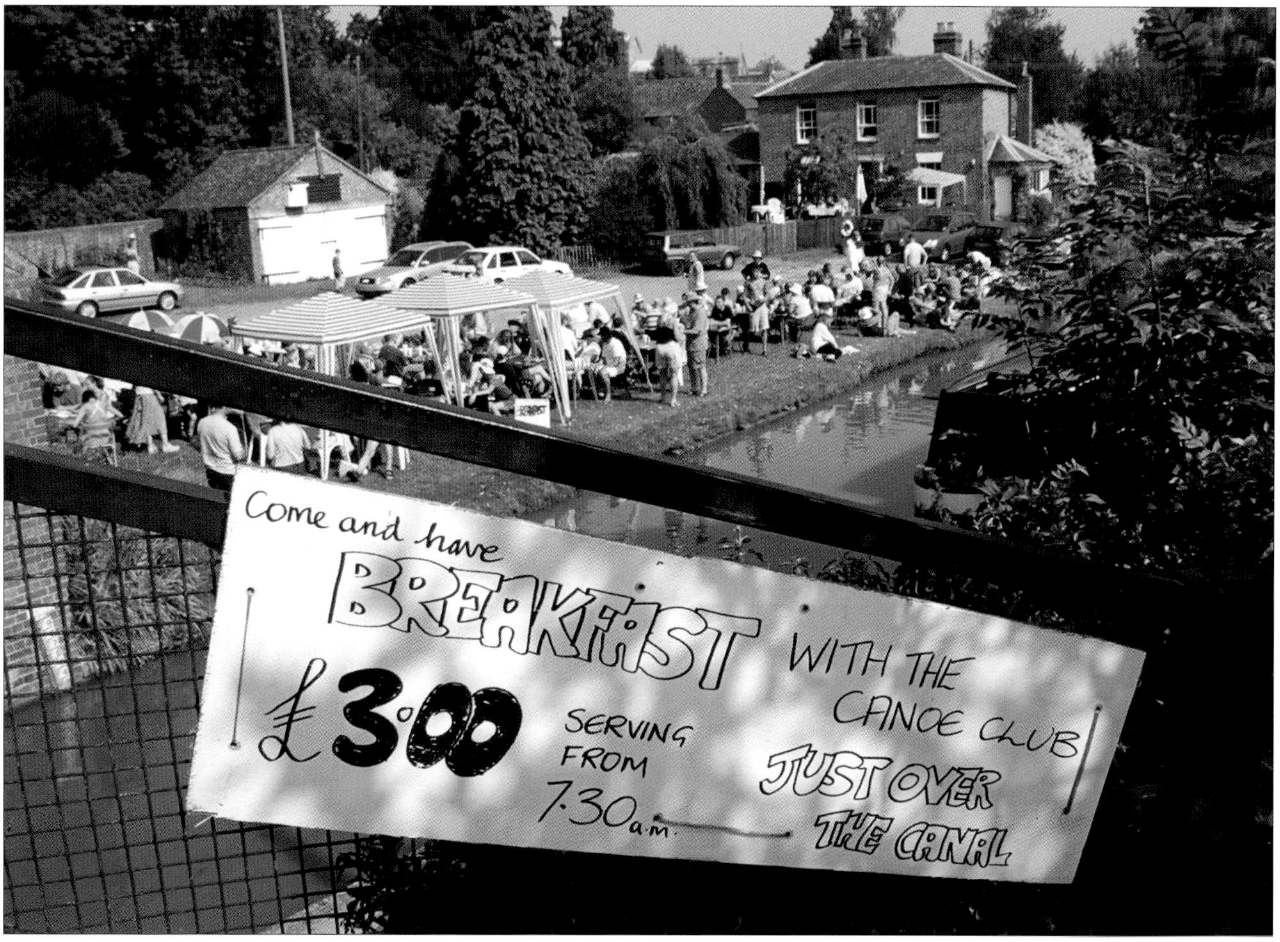

2003
2003

Come rain
come shine
it's always fine
with
Fairport
Convention

2003
2004|2003

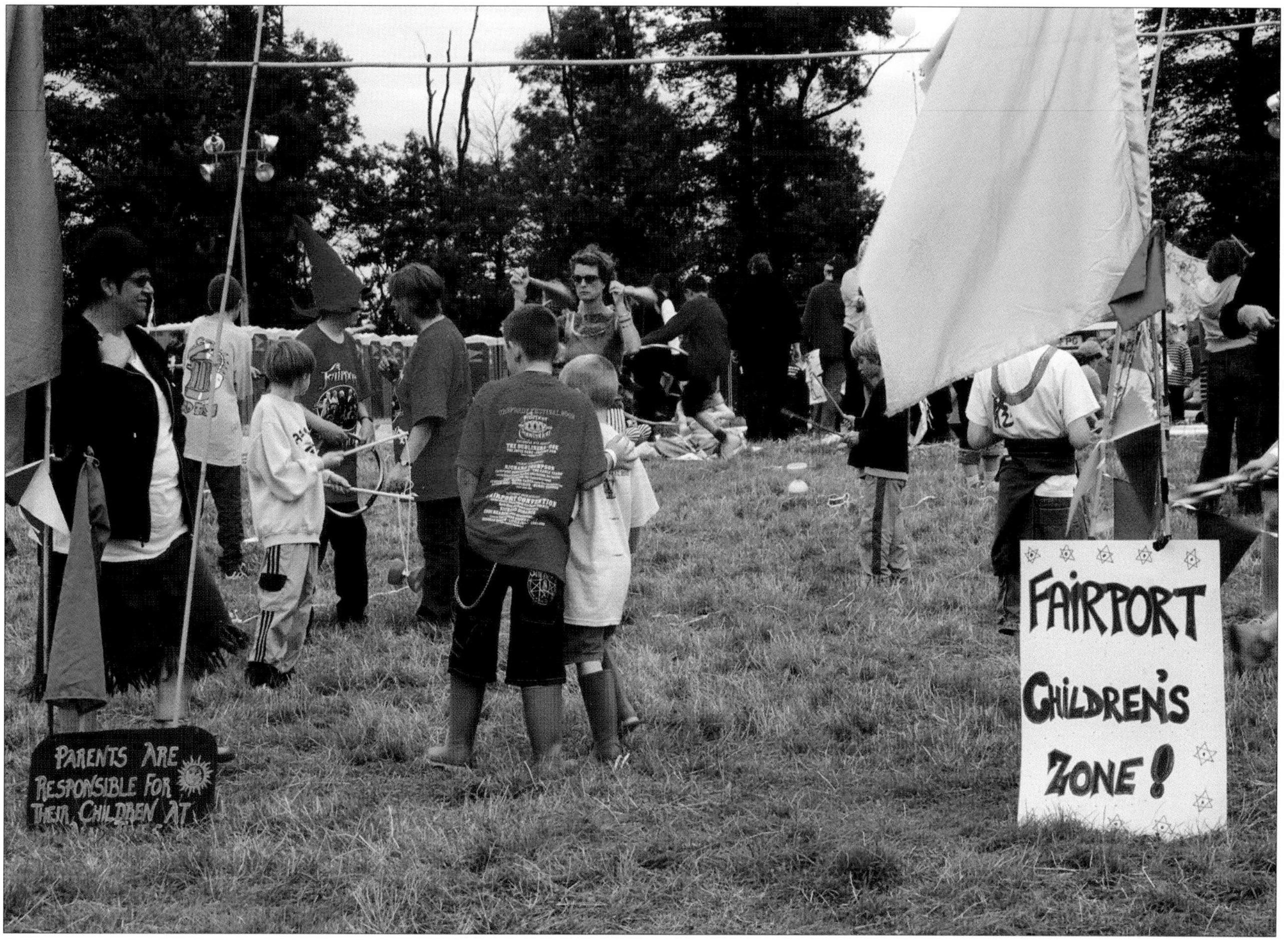

2002
1996

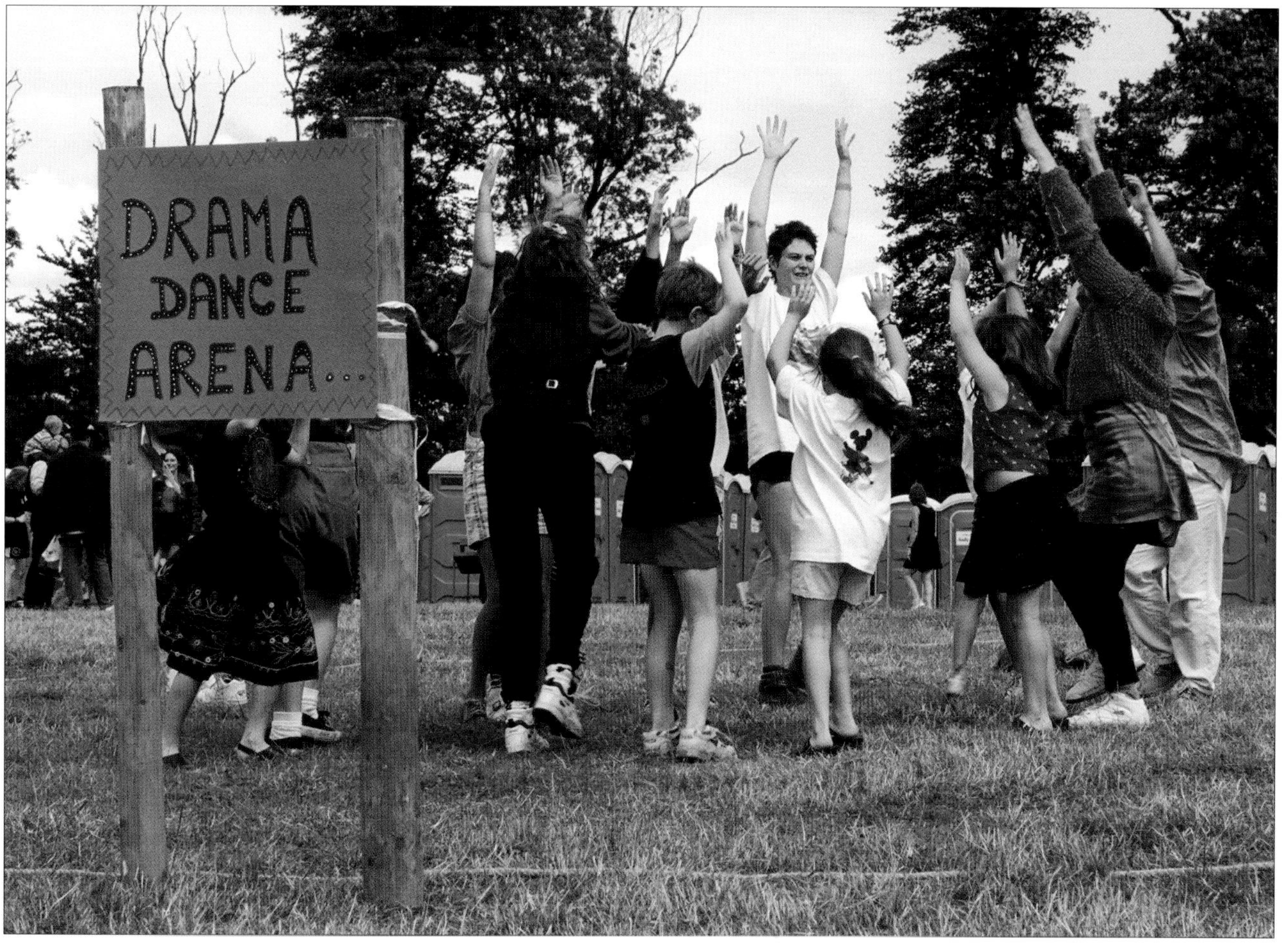

1999	1996
2002	
2002	2002

2002
2002

2002
2002|2001

2002|2000
2002|1999

2004

Festival Style Themes

T-shirts pages 56-59

Tattoos pages 60-61

Hair pages 62-65

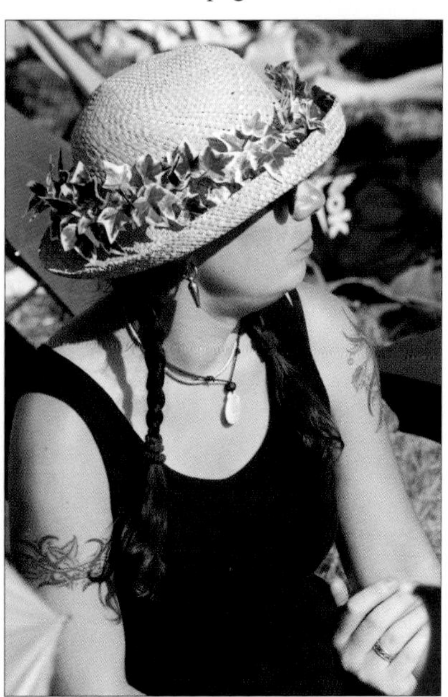

Hats pages 66-70

Bracelets pages 71-73

Beards pages 74-76

2004
2004 | 2004 | 2004
2002

Jerry Donahue
Fairport Convention
Edward II
Chris Leslie
The Richard Thompson Band
Joe Brown and his Band
1996 Cropredy Festival

Roy Wood's Army
Edward II
Fairport Convention
Loudon Wainwright III

CROPREDY FESTIVAL
CROPREDY 1999

Fairport Convention

1996

2004		2004
2004	2003	2003
2003	1994	2002

2004|2003
2003

2004|2003
2001

2002

1994
2000 | 1999

2001 | 1999
2000 | 2000

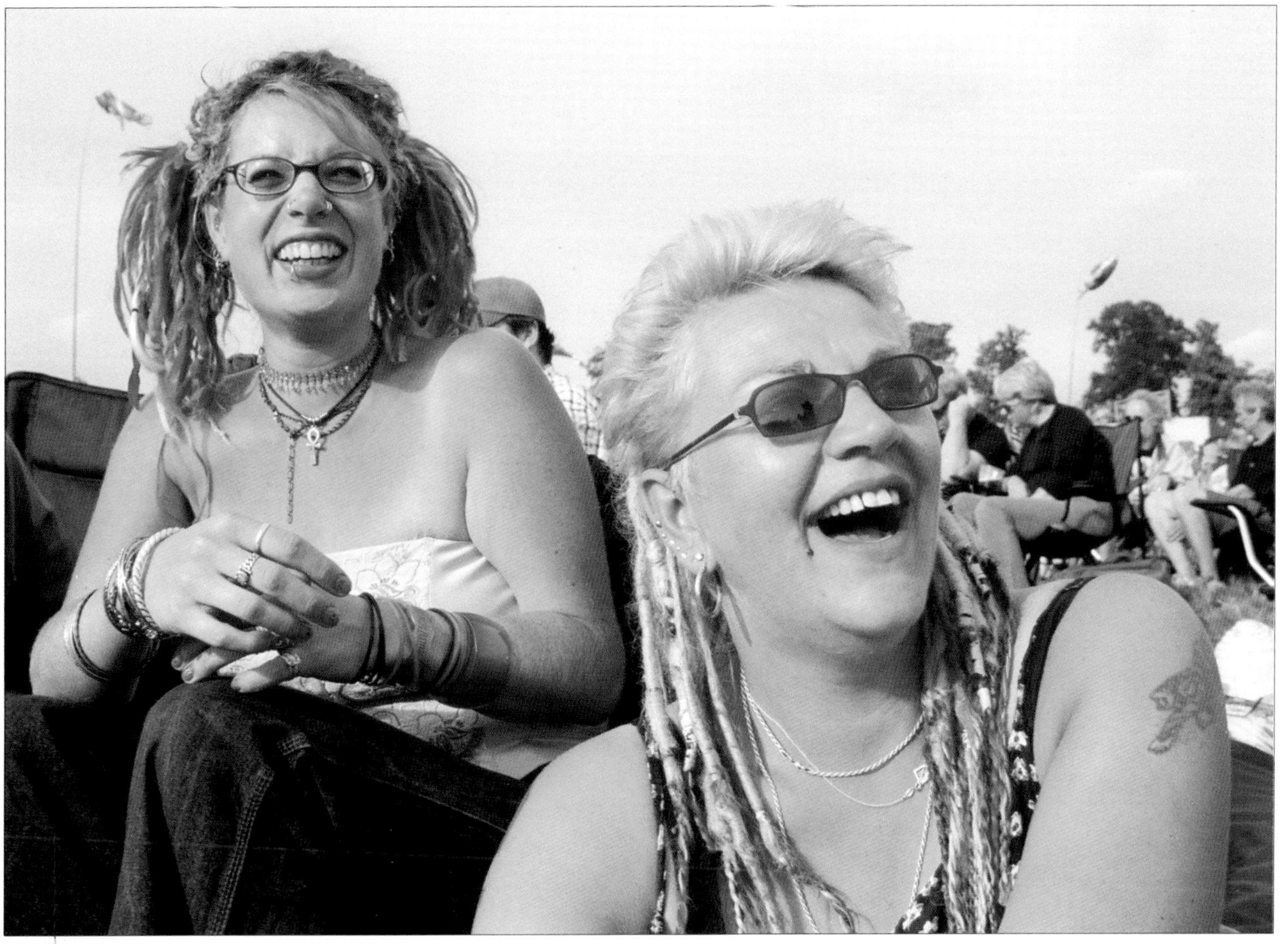

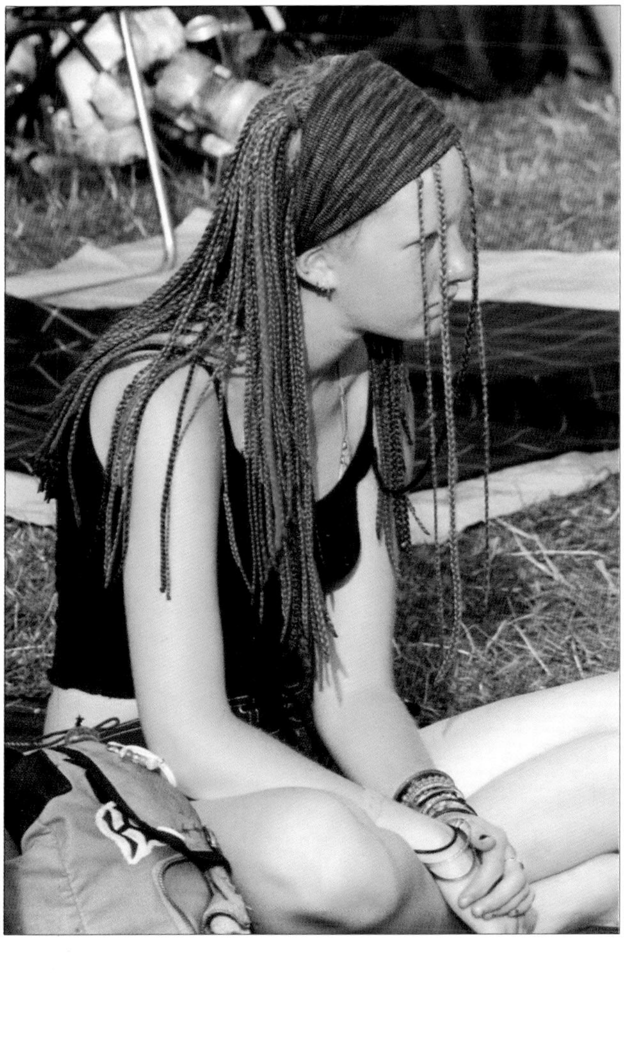

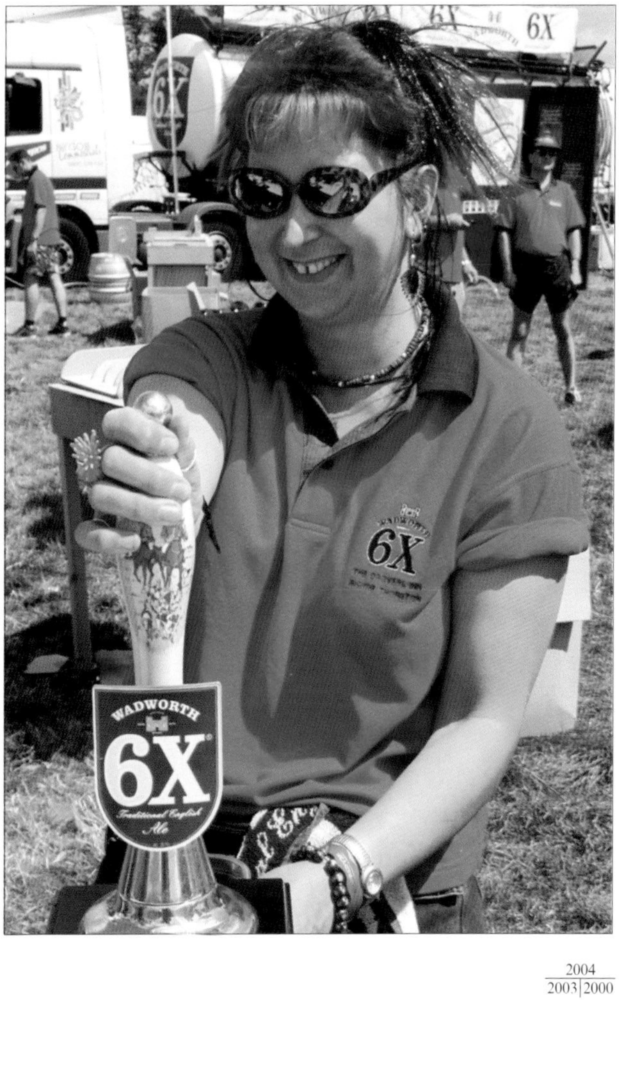
WADWORTH
6X
Traditional English Ale

2004
2003|2000

2003

2003|2003
2003|1999

2004|2003
2002

	1995	
2002	1999	2003
	2000	

2003

2004

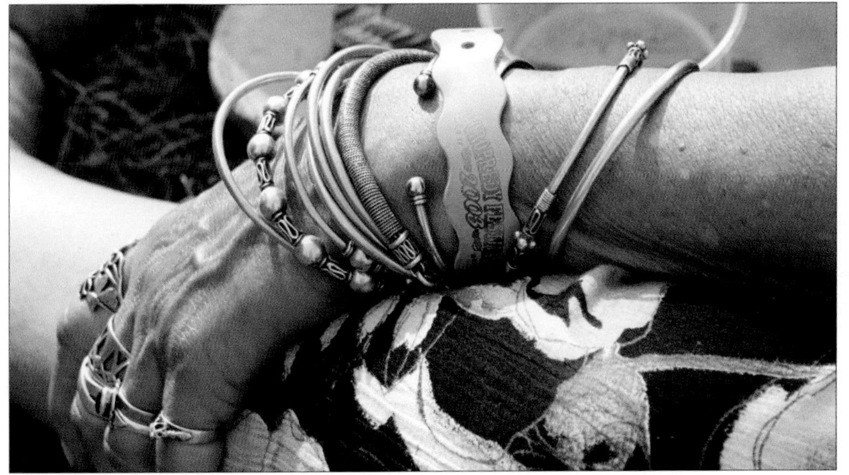

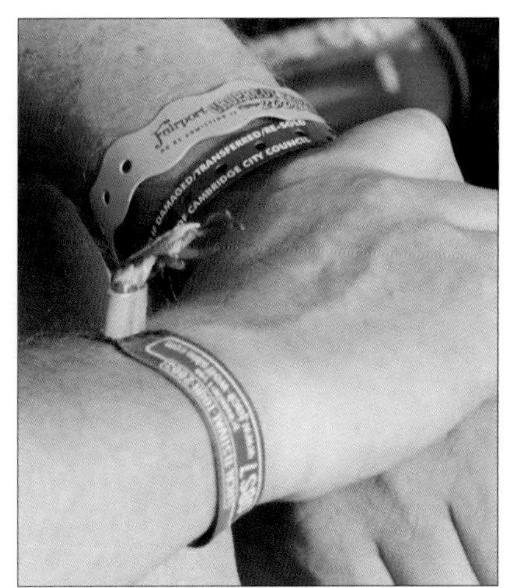

2004
2003

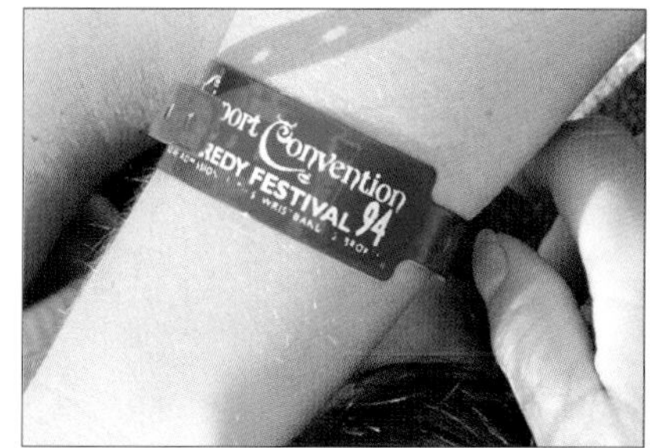

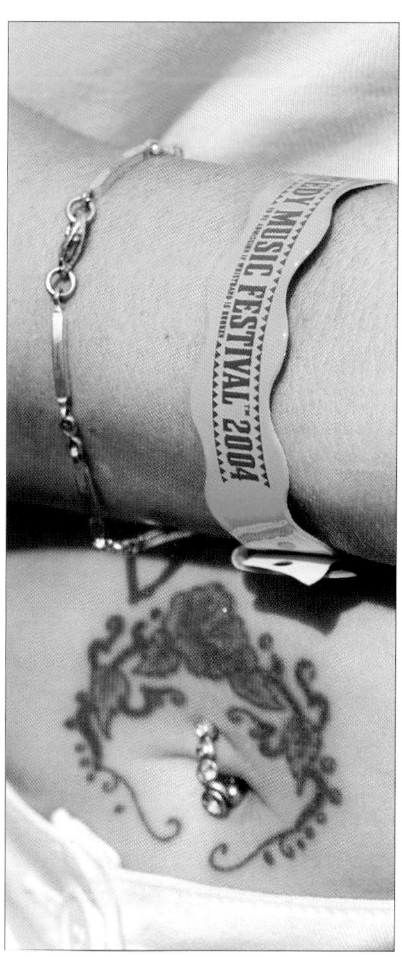

2003	2000
1994-2003	2004
2004	

2004	2003
1998	2002

2002	2004
2003	1999

BAZZA
BAZZA
CROPREDY FESTIVAL
2003
THURSDAY 7th AUGUST
FRIDAY 8th AUGUST AND
SATURDAY 9th AUGUST
Fairport Convention
6X
WADWORTH
Great Beers at Cropredy

2004

Style on Stage

Mundy-Turner '02 | Anna Ryder '03

Robert Plant '00 | Martin Carthy & Dave Pegg '03
Ric Sanders '03 | Mostly Autumn '04 | Maartin Allcock '03
Fairport friends '04 | Richard Thompson '97

Robert Plant 2000

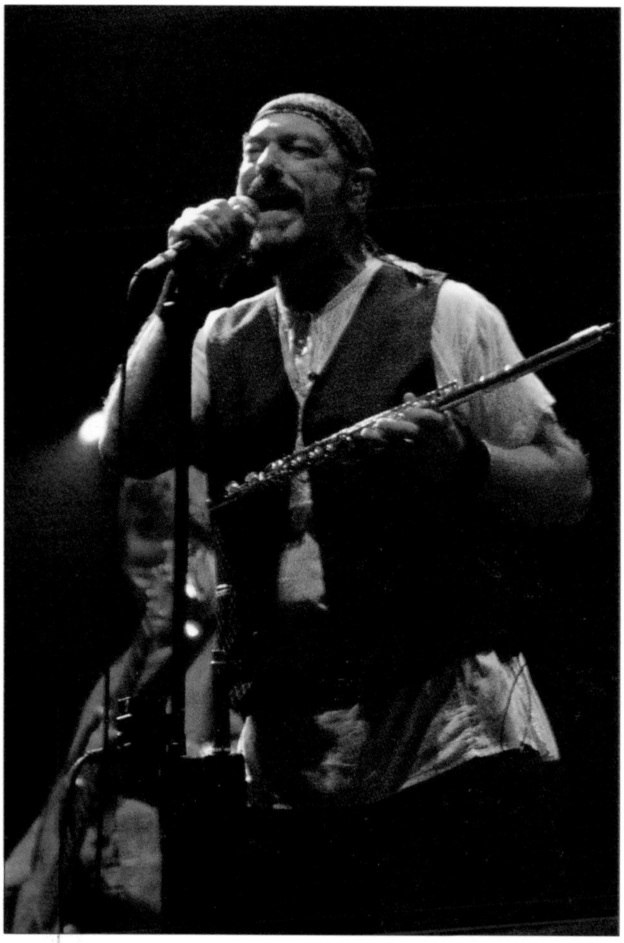

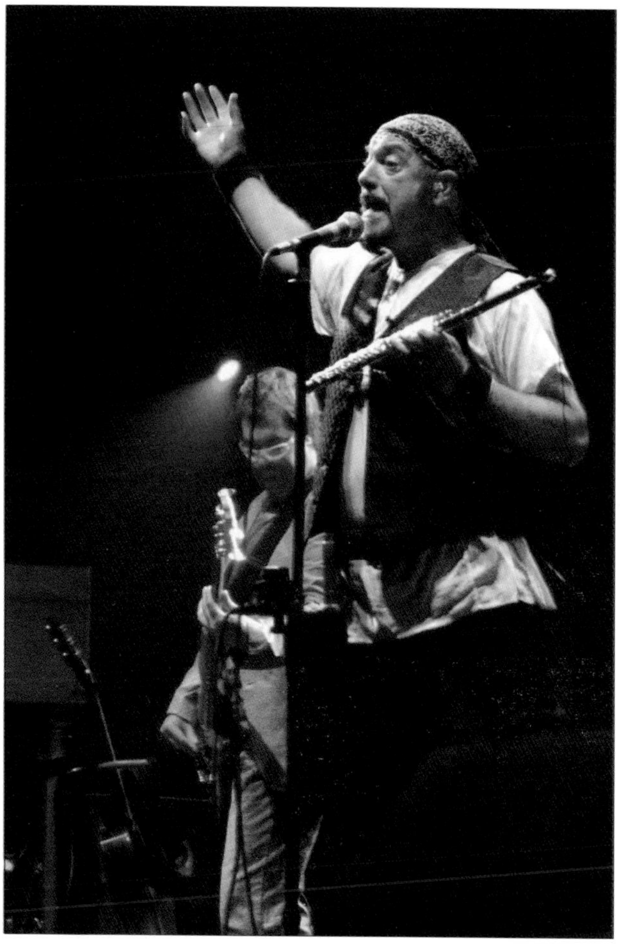

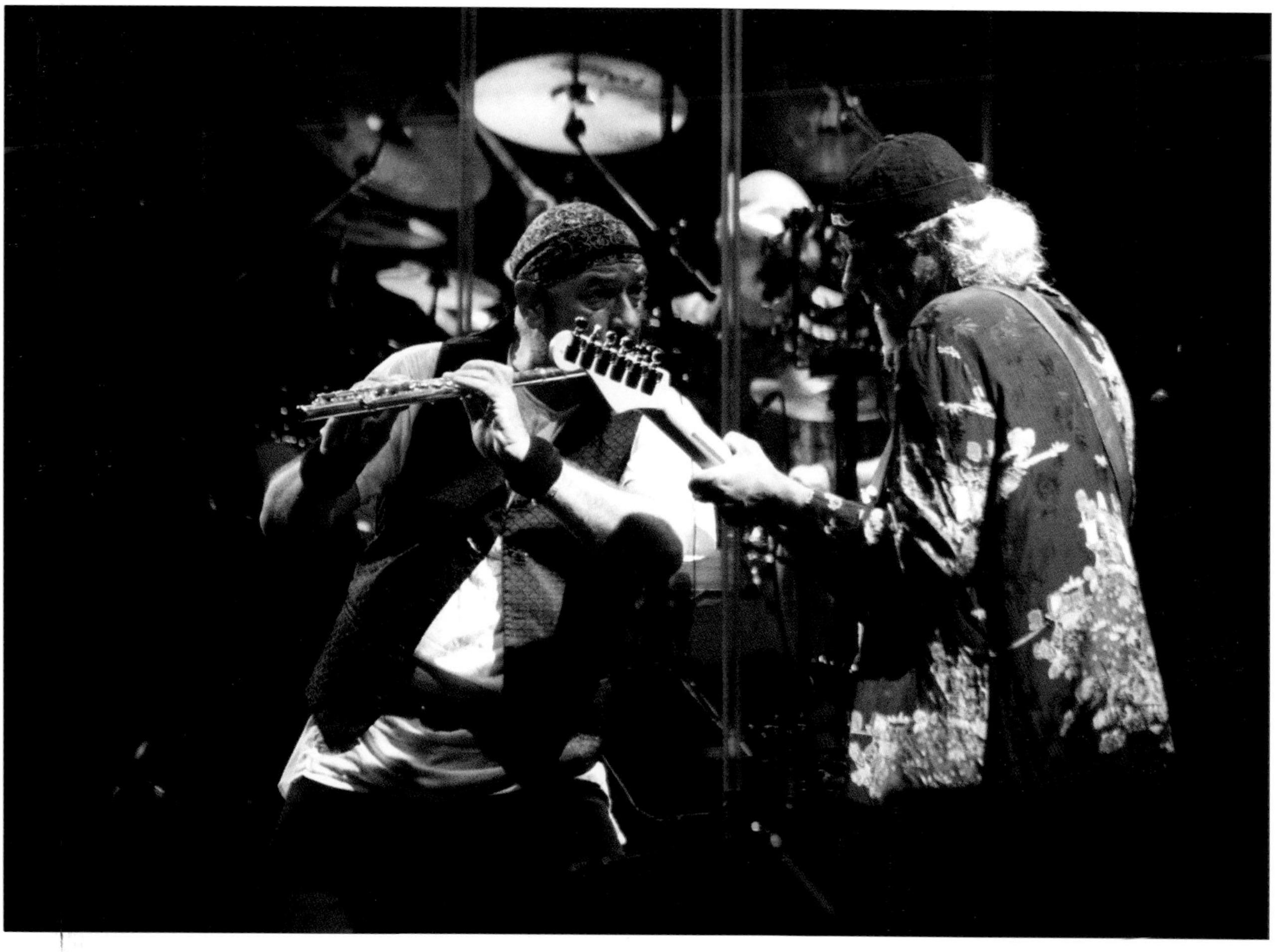

Jethro Tull 2004

Kathryn Tickell '95	Waulk Electric '95	Barrage '99
Sandwitch '01	Blodwyn Pig '94	Equation '03
Sandwitch '01	Liam Genockey '01	

Anna Ryder 1998

Man (Deke Leonard) 1994

Mostly Autumn '04	Solstice '98
Barrage '99	Equation '03

Eliza Carthy '01 | Norma Waterson & Martin Carthy '01
Eliza Carthy Band '01

Eddi Reader & Jacqui McShee '99
Maddy Prior '99 | Julianne Regan '00

Maartin Allcock 2001

Maartin Allcock 2003

Beryl Marriott '03 | David Hughes '03
Robin Williamson '00
Julie Matthews '03 | Chris While '03

Vikki Clayton '01
Vikki Clayton '97 | Vikki Clayton '98

Dave Swarbrick 1997

Dave Swarbrick 1997

Ashley Hutchings '97 | Ashley Hutchings '02
Ashley Hutchings '04 | Morris Dancers '04

Albion Band '00
Tommy Connolly Dancers '97

Richard Thompson 2002

Judy Dyble 1997

Jerry Donahue '04 | Iain Matthews '02
Dave Mattacks '97 | Jerry Donahue & Iain Matthews '00

Gerry Conway '99 | Gerry Conway '03
Gerry Conway '02

Simon Nicol 1994

Simon Nicol '03 | Simon Nicol '97
Richard Thompson & Simon Nicol '97

Ric Sanders 1994

Ric Sanders '00

Ric Sanders & Chris Leslie '04

Dave Pegg 1994

Dave Pegg '00

Simon Nicol & Dave Pegg '99 | Dave Pegg '97

Chris Leslie '00 | Chris Leslie '01
Ric Sanders & Chris Leslie '01

Chris Leslie 2003

Simon, Vikki & Dave 1994

Simon Nicol & Steve Gibbons '03

Kevin Dempsey, John Kirkpatrick & Dave Pegg '04

Fairport Convention, family & friends 2004

"Goodnight, God bless, same time, same place, next year"

Simon Nicol